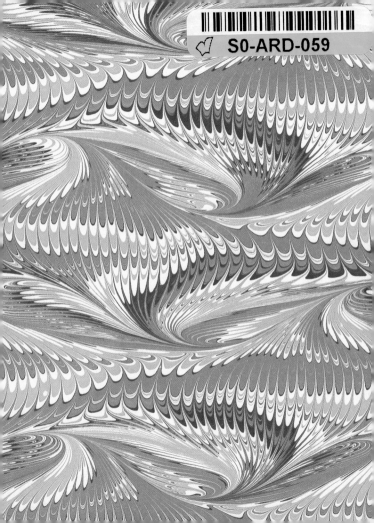

S0-ARD-059

# LOVING THOUGHTS
## *for*
## Health and Healing

---

## Louise L. Hay

---

Hay House
Carson, California

Library of Congress Cataloging-in-Publication Data
Hay, Louise L.
    Loving thoughts for health and healing / Louise L. Hay.
        p.    cm.
    ISBN 1-56170-070-3 : $5.95
    1. Health. 2. Affirmations. 3. Self-care, Health. I. Title.
RA776.5.H34   1993
613--dc20                                              93-13177
                                                            CIP

Design & Typesetting by: Michele Lanci-Altomare

93 94 95 96 97 98   10 9 8 7 6 5 4 3 2 1
First Printing, September 1993

Published and Distributed in the United States by:
Hay House, Inc.
P.O. Box 6204
Carson, CA 90749-6204

Printed in the United States of America
on Recycled Paper

# INTRODUCTION

The power of positive thinking is a well-known healing force even within the medical community. The positive, loving thoughts on the following pages are nothing more than positive affirmations.

You may feel that thinking a positive thought cannot possibly change your life, but how many times have you repeatedly affirmed a negative thought about yourself until finally it became true for you? Why not change those negative thoughts to positive ones?

I like to compare positive affirmations to planting a seed. You don't just plant the seed and get a beautiful flower the next day. It takes time. First you must water and nurture the seed and make sure it is safe from harm. It is the same with positive affirmations. You may not see changes immediately, but with enough nurturing and encouragement you can change your old negative way of thinking and look at things in a new and positive light.

Use these affirmations daily and over time you will begin to see your life turn in new direction and you will reap a bountiful harvest of positive, loving endeavors for yourself.

All is well,

*Louise L. Hay*

# Today...

I choose
to be happy,
healthy and whole.

# Today...

is
the time
for healing.

# Today...

I listen with love
to my own body's
messages.

# Today...

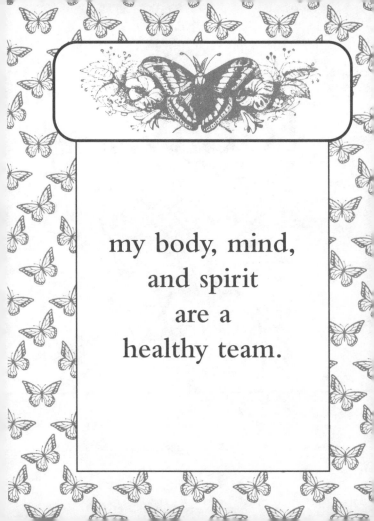

my body, mind,
and spirit
are a
healthy team.

# Today...

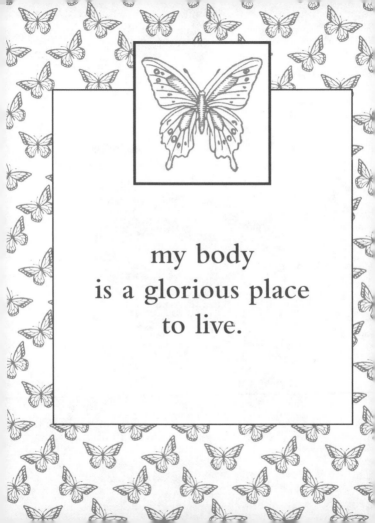

my body
is a glorious place
to live.

# Today...

I open my heart
and allow
my healing gifts
to flow.

# Today...

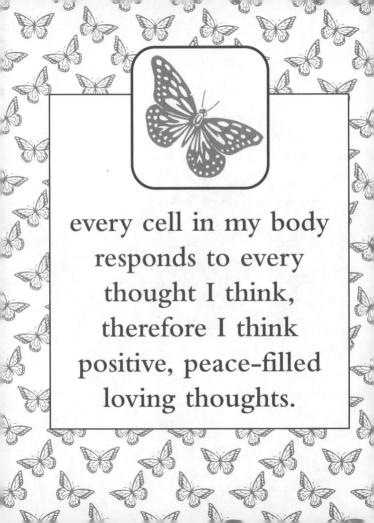

every cell in my body
responds to every
thought I think,
therefore I think
positive, peace-filled
loving thoughts.

# Today...

I remember
to breathe deeply
and to fully relax
my body and mind
often during
the day.

# Today...

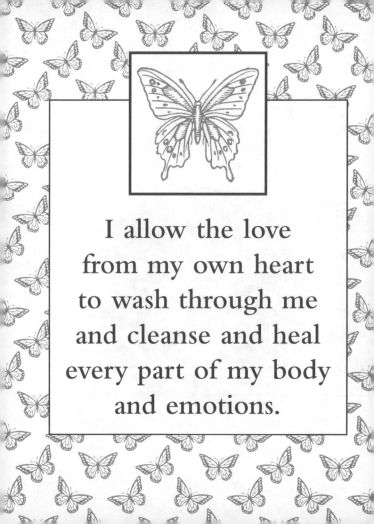

I allow the love
from my own heart
to wash through me
and cleanse and heal
every part of my body
and emotions.

# Today...

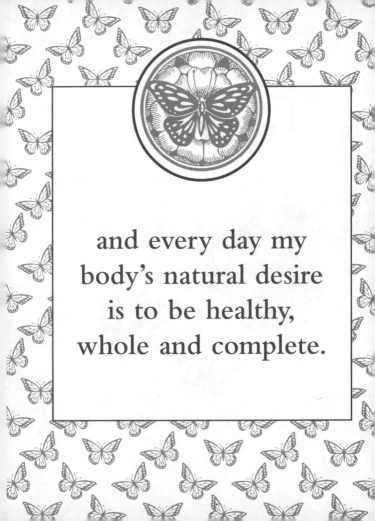

and every day my
body's natural desire
is to be healthy,
whole and complete.

# Today...

I feel glorious,
dynamic energy
within me.

# Today...

and every day
my health
is getting better
all the time.

# Today...

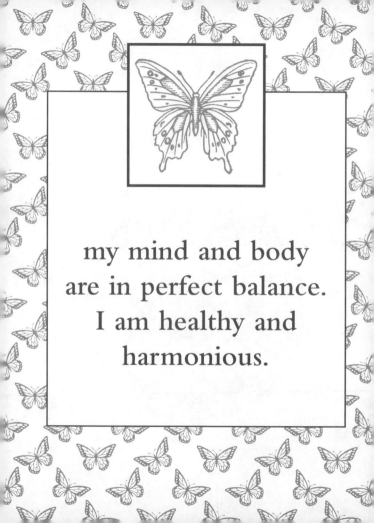

my mind and body
are in perfect balance.
I am healthy and
harmonious.

# Today...

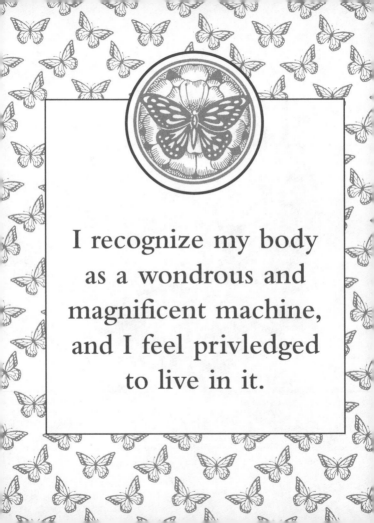

I recognize my body
as a wondrous and
magnificent machine,
and I feel privledged
to live in it.

# Today...

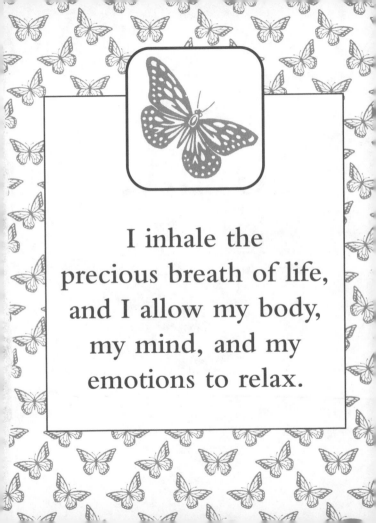

I inhale the
precious breath of life,
and I allow my body,
my mind, and my
emotions to relax.

# Today...

I look terrific
and I feel
terrific.

# Today...

it gives me joy
to take loving care
of myself.

# Today...

I approve
of my body
exactly as it is.

# Today...

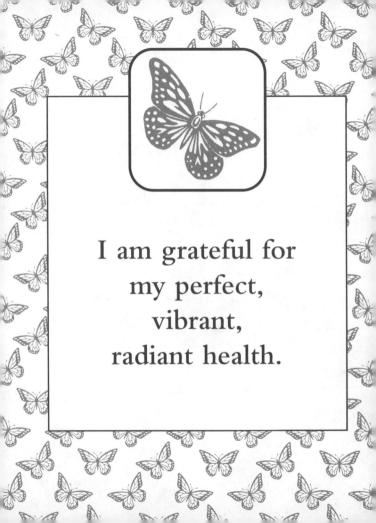

I am grateful for
my perfect,
vibrant,
radiant health.

# Today...

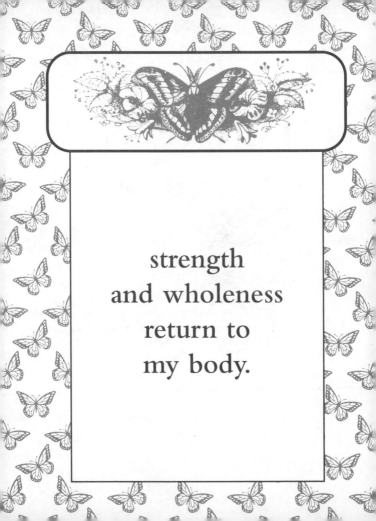

strength
and wholeness
return to
my body.

# Today...

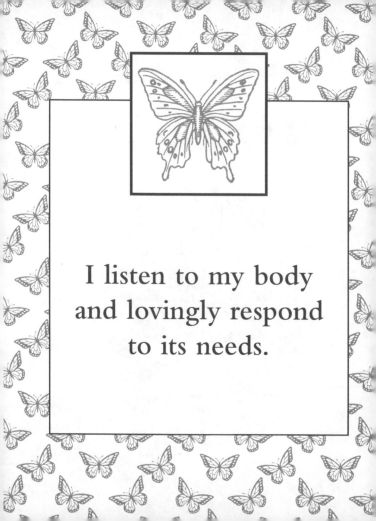

I listen to my body
and lovingly respond
to its needs.

# Today...

I know
I am worth
healing.

# Today...

I have a wonderful, loving relationship with my health practitioner.

# Today...

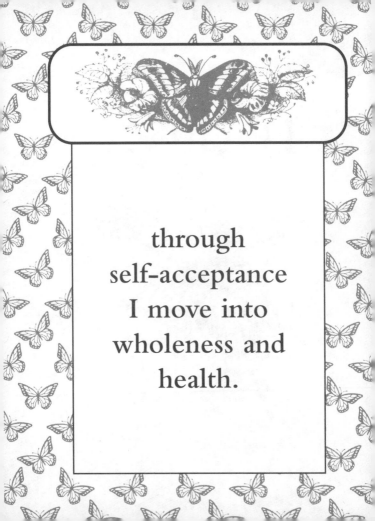

through
self–acceptance
I move into
wholeness and
health.

# Today...

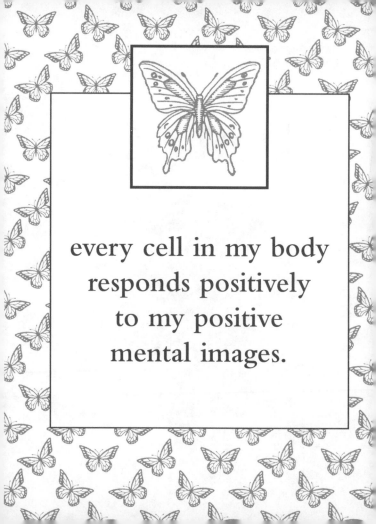

every cell in my body
responds positively
to my positive
mental images.

# Today...

vibrant health is
my constant
companion.

# Today...

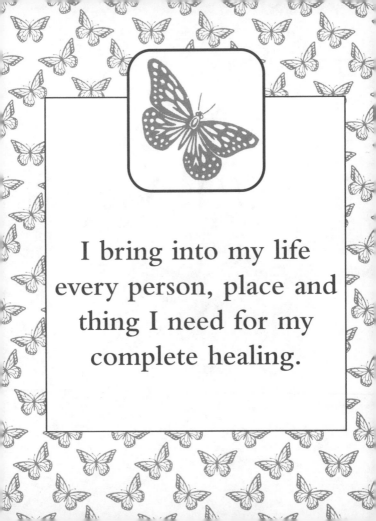

I bring into my life every person, place and thing I need for my complete healing.

# Today...

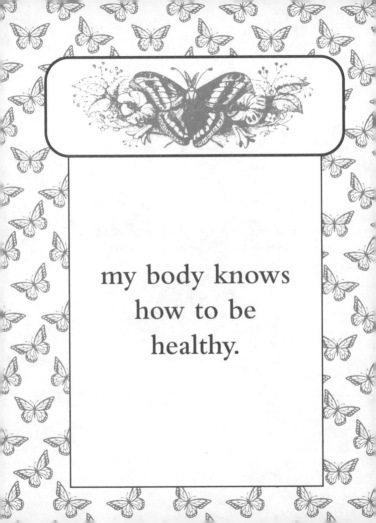

my body knows
how to be
healthy.

# Today...

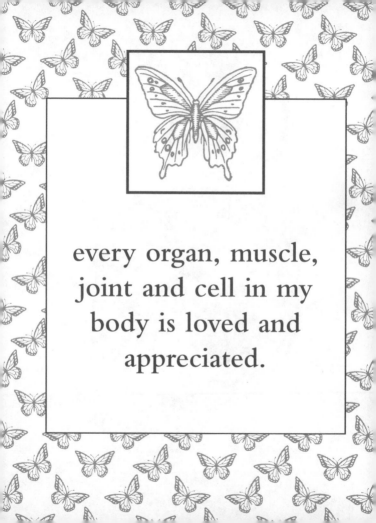

every organ, muscle,
joint and cell in my
body is loved and
appreciated.

# Today...